Dedication

For a cat named Catwallader, a parakeet named Lindbird, the fencing team at Sing Sing, the debating society at Vassar, and all those who think they could have done it better. Oh, and of course, for the one pretty special to behold.

Published by LONGSTREET PRESS, INC.
a subsidiary of Cox Newspapers,
a subsidiary of Cox Enterprises, Inc.
2140 Newmarket Parkway
Suite 122
Marietta, Georgia 30067

Printed in the United States of America

1st printing 1997

Library of Congress Card Catalog Number 96-79793

ISBN: 1-56352-384-1

Book design by Jill Dible
Jacket design by Graham & Company Graphics

Thankful

FURMAN BISHER

LONGSTREET PRESS
Atlanta, Georgia

Introduction

This book is for people who enjoy the little things in life, but sometimes take them for granted. If you're like me, you need to be reminded, more than once a year, of the small joys that make life (literally) wonderful.

Nobody took giving thanks more seriously than the Pilgrims, who were so grateful they'd survived their first New England winter in 1623, that they spent three days getting the victuals ready to celebrate with their new friends, the Indians.

That seems to have been the signal for the rest of us, down through the years. "It [Thanksgiving] calls up memories of kitchens and pantries crowded with good things to eat," it is written in my encyclopedia. ". . . also religious thinking, church services, and prayer." There was nothing official about the holiday until President Lincoln proclaimed it so in 1863, "a day of thanksgiving and praise to our beneficent Father," while we were in the middle of a war amongst ourselves.

Just about a century later I got caught up in the spirit of the season, but for a different reason. I had become a father for the first time and it was an experience that brought appreciation for a lot of things bubbling up to the surface. I inaugurated then a Thanksgiving column that has been a hard habit to break.

I have sometimes been thankful seriously, I have sometimes been thankful for the most curious things, and at other times I have merely pulled somebody's leg. One year I veered from the course. I wrote of things I wasn't thankful for, and the backlash was severe. People wrote that I had wounded a warm spirit that I had established, and that I should have been ashamed. I was. I never did it again

— not that I wasn't tempted.

For example, it's pretty hard to consider the Atlanta Falcons and be thankful. It's hard to hit my tee shot into the lake and be thankful. It's hard to be thankful when your wife is 45 minutes late. It's hard to be thankful when the bug inspector says you've got termites. It's hard to hook a two-pound bass, see him slip off your line, and be thankful. . . .

But experience has taught me that it warms more hearts to be positive than negative, even with a twist of humor or a pull of the leg. That being the case, after all these years, I've tried to pull my thoughts together and assemble those of a related nature under a kind of heading that tells you what to expect. Some are dated, some are updated, and most are just for the fun of it.

Be thankful, not just at Thanksgiving. Any time of the year is a good time to be grateful.

— FURMAN BISHER

Home
and
Hearth

*I'm thankful we haven't had
to put our fallout shelter to use.*

*at the sight of smoke rising
from a chimney on a crisp day.*

*for the dog that knows the difference
between a stranger and a friend.*

*for the repairman who says,
"I'll be right over."*

*the kind of grass I deal with
is mowed, not smoked.*

↬

for the warmth of flickering firelight.

↬

*when the noise in the night
turns out to be the icemaker.*

↬

*for the mailman, the garbage man
and the man who delivers my
newspaper — on the porch,
not under the shrubbery.*

for the busying around and the fragrances in the kitchen during holiday season.

✎

when the power comes back on.

✎

for twilight in the winter, when lights begin flickering on in kitchen windows.

for that first blast of air conditioning when it's blistering outside.

❧

for the notice from the bank that says I can burn the mortgage.

❧

when my wife comes home from the hairdresser and I can say "That looks really good" without lying.

❧

for a good rocking chair.

*the school bus passes my house
and doesn't stop anymore.*

*for the way rain makes
you glad to be inside.*

*when last year's Christmas
tree lights still work.*

Life on the Road

*for the airline pilot who realizes
we came along for the ride,
not for comedy hour.*

*for "blue highways" that
lead you to the real America.*

*when the pilot can say it's bright and
beautiful where we're going.*

*when the passenger in the next seat
doesn't try to talk through my nap.*

*for the cab driver who spares me
his political views.*

*when the traffic backup is on the
other side of the expressway.*

*for the sight of a gas station when
I've been driving too long on "E."*

*when the 18-wheeler behind me
concedes that there is room on the
interstate for both of us.*

*when the traffic light turns green
just as I get there.*

*for the first streaks of dawn after
I've been flying all night.*

*for the downy comfort of my
own bed after a long road trip.*

People
and
Music

*for the sound of a
barbershop quartet.*

❧

*for Eddie Haywood at the piano.
(You get it only second hand now.)
He grew up in Atlanta and
his greatest gift was
"Canadian Sunset."*

❧

*for "September Song,"
a theme song of sorts for
some of us graybeards.*

*for the screeching, tormented
sound of a rock band — when it stops.*

✧

*for the strains of "Auld Lang
Syne" on New Year's Eve,
especially Guy Lombardo's way.*

✧

Bing came along in my time.

✧

*for the brassy blast of a college band
splitting the air on a Saturday
afternoon at the stadium.*

for the old "big band" sound.

*we haven't had an album of
Jerry Glanville's biggest hits.*

for music I can pat my foot to.

*for the skirl of bagpipes, even if
they do sound like something
in need of oiling.*

*for the Buffalo Bills (the ones
who sang harmony, not the ones who
lost all those Super Bowl games).*

*for Perry Como, who makes it
sound so easy.*

*for the pealing little voices
of a children's choir.*

for classical music (even though
I can't pat my foot to it).

for Tennessee Ernie and "16 Tons."

for the band that plays the kind of
music that brings us closer together,
especially the two of us.

for Christmas music,
after Thanksgiving.

Food and Drink

*for a dish of collards, cooked by
somebody who knows how collards
ought to be fixed.*

sweet potato isn't our national pie.

*when the roadside restaurant
I happen onto turns out to be
a joyful surprise.*

*for the fragrance that tells me
there's a cake in the oven.*

*for the first gulp of
cold milk on a hot summer day.*

*for a hamburger with
a slice of onion on top.*

*for the sizzle of a steak
over a charcoal fire.*

*for the aroma of frying bacon
and brewing coffee.*

*when I don't have to mortgage the
house to pay the dinner bill.*

‰

*for the kind of chilli that makes your
head break out in a sweat.*

‰

*for ice cream — strawberry, vanilla,
chocolate, 28 flavors, 31 flavors,
homemade, store-bought, cone,
cup, carton, or barrel.*

Antiquity

I can remember the time when you turned the phone crank and talked to "central."

there's a Wrigley Field and a Fenway Park, and I'm sorry there will no longer be an Atlanta Stadium.

when I'm out jogging and the other guy turns out to be another graybeard.

for the scratchy sound of an old Glenn Miller wax.

my folks never sent me off to camp. (Who am I kidding? Only camp I ever heard of around our village was prison camp.)

I came along in a time when men didn't call other men "baby."

I can remember when "gay" was just an adjective.

when the old building gets a refurbishing and not the demolition ball.

for those people who age, but don't grow old.

*for what the old 4-letter athlete stood
for— a nice 4-letter word like* "hero."

the Atlanta Journal *still*
"*covers Dixie like the dew,*"
if only on the masthead.

*I came along in the
age of the typewriter.*

*I'm old enough to appreciate
the young and young enough to
appreciate the old.*

Parental Joys
and
Hazards

*for the sound of the car pulling
into the driveway after one of mine
has been out on his first date.*

*for the little voice at the other end of
the table toiling through the blessing.*

*when my guy scrambles up from
the pile after the play is over.*

*for the willing voice that says,
"Can I help you, Daddy?"*

*when one of mine
brags on his brother.*

*for the driver who actually slows
down when he sees a sign that says
"Slow – Children."*

*for the fresh, clean fragrance
of a babe in arms.*

*for young people who know how to
say "sir" and "ma'am."*

for a good report card.

for the peace and quiet that falls over the house after all the young ones have been bedded down.

when the telephone rings and it's one of my brood who hasn't been heard from lately—even if he needs something.

"O, Say
Can You
See . . ."

for the sight of an academy cadet,
shoulders back, chin up,
giving grace to the uniform.

I got no closer to the shooting
than Midway Island.

for that one moment of total peace
when the national anthem rings out
across the stadium just before kickoff
and that I can sing along with it.

for politicians. (May as well be, we're going to have them anyway.)

❧

I've been to the Normandy beaches and seen how it happened there, something I think every American should see.

❧

the United States of America has made it the first 200 years, (but I don't envy those who have to go the next 200).

for national holidays, for that's the one time people seem to stop and take a good look at their blessings.

for a visit to Yorktown, which I can recommend to any American who'd like a better understanding of the founding fathers.

we're not fighting another war with anybody about anything.

Sort of
Personal

more thankful for "fall back" than "spring forward," but I'd be even happier if they'd leave the clock alone and let the sun tell time.

for the warm, sweaty feeling after a morning jog — makes me feel so wholesome.

for the prayer that leaves a little room for insertions of my own.

*for April and October, two great
months to be on a golf course.*

when my checking account balances.

*when the weather tells me it's time
for the first wearing of the tweeds.*

*aging isn't nearly as bad as
it looked when I was 18.*

I don't have to call some radio psychologist to get my problems solved.

for the cool of winter, but I'm not so hot for the heat of summer.

for pay day.

*for zippers, (and you will be,
too, the older you get).*

❧

*for my partner in life, who, thank
heaven, has a sense of humor and
is pretty special to behold.*

❧

*when my clothes come back from
the cleaner in the same shape
I left them, only cleaner.*

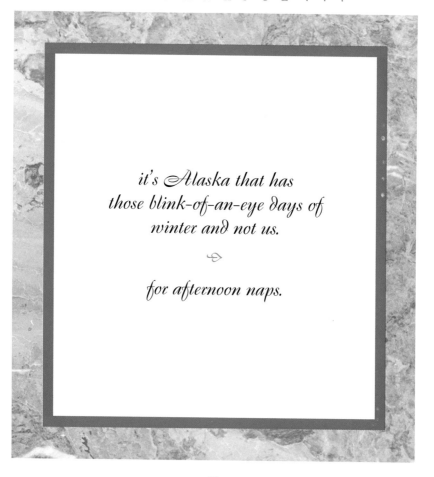

it's Alaska that has
those blink-of-an-eye days of
winter and not us.

for afternoon naps.

Manners

*for the lady who still expects
to have the door opened for her.*

for the guy who still opens it.

*to get to the nut line tray before
somebody else has picked out
all the cashews.*

when somebody at work says,
"Hey, nice job."

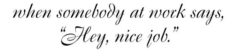

for the old grad who's willing to
admit, after losing the game, that
there might be something worthy
about the other school.

*for the traveler who uses the litter
barrel and not the side of the
highway for his garbage.*

*for the smoker who notices that
the sign says "No Smoking."*

*for the football player
who hands the ball to the official
after he scores.*

*when a caller has the manners to
apologize for a wrong number.*

*for the schoolboy
who remembers my name.*

❧

*for the lady who remembers that the
most important thing about being a
woman is being a lady.*

Sights, Sounds & Smells

for the pure, forgiving sound of a church bell on Sunday morning.

for the reverence that falls over a football stadium when the crowd stands and sings the alma mater.

when the old diesel fires up on a frigid morning.

for the frozen pose of a bird dog on point.

*for long, shady home-lined
streets that you seem to see only in
small towns anymore.*

*for the first clap of thunder after
we've had a long dry spell.*

*for the silence a snowfall seems to
bring over the land.*

*for music drifting through
an open window.*

*when the sound of the
dentist's drill stops.*

*for the sound of a congregation
singing as I near the church on a
Sunday morning, even though it
means I'm a little late.*

*for the sound of golf spikes
on a walkway.*

*for that part of a speech that goes,
"And in conclusion . . . ."*

The
Sporting
Side

*I saw Jack Dempsey box,
Eddie Arcaro ride, Shoeless Joe
Jackson bat and Cy Young pitch.
(No kidding.)*

*I saw Ted Turner manage,
but not for long, thank heaven.*

*Richard Petty retired in time,
and in one piece.*

for the old prize fighter
whose nose and ears don't give
away his former career.

❧

I got to spend some time in
Bobby Jones's company, but
I'm sorry I was too late to see
him swing at a golf ball.

❧

for Gene Sarazen, my version of a
sportsman, and long may he wave.

*I got to see Bobby Dodd work a
sideline on a Saturday afternoon.*

*for the athlete who decides
not to write a book about it.*

*when the lost ball turns up –
playable – just as you're about to
give up the search.*

*for the coach who concedes that he
only is No. 2 – to God.*

*for the gifted athlete who
realizes that what he has is only
borrowed, and some day he'll
have to give it all back.*

✧

*for the Heisman Trophy,
though mildly so; I'd prefer they
reserve it for seniors.*

✧

*the Olympic Games have come and
gone, and as for you, Señor Juan
Antonio Samaranch, don't slam
the door on your way out.*

for a picnic on a grassy slope
before the big game.

for the final second on the clock
when our team is in the lead.

for 20-game winners and pitchers
who go 9 innings.

*for that "clunk" of the putt
that drops.*

*for the golfer who cares enough
to repair the ball mark and rake
the bunker.*

*for "walk-ons" who go out
for the team and make it.*

for the sight of a little ol' jockey on the back of a big ol' horse running like the wind, passing everything down the stretch.

for St. Andrews, but if it were over here, some Americans would say, "I've played golf in better cow pastures."